EXPLORE THE WILD WEST

PATHFINDER EDITION

By Brian LaFleur and Shirleyann Costigan

CONTENTS

Forgotten
COWBOYS

African American cowboys were tough, they were brave, and a few even became famous. Yet history forgot about them for many years.

✦ By Brian LaFleur ✦

In the early days of the American West, being a cowboy was a tough job. Cowboys moved herds of cattle over long distances, and they also tamed and rode wild horses. The life of a cowboy was exciting, but it was also dangerous.

Still, lots of people became cowboys. There might have been about 100,000 cowboys in all. They came from a variety of cultural backgrounds, but more than half of all cowboys were either Mexican or African American. Let's look more closely at African American cowboy history.

Many African Americans moved west after the **Civil War**, the war that made them free, ended in 1865. Newly freed people often moved in search of better lives, and so, by 1890, nearly 100,000 African American men, women, and children lived in Texas and Oklahoma alone. There they looked for jobs.

Newly freed people had a hard time finding jobs in the West. They experienced **discrimination**, or unequal treatment, and often they could only find the hardest jobs, so that's why many became cowboys.

Because of their bravery, some hardworking cowboys became famous, and writers often wrote books about them. Some cowboys wrote books about themselves. A book about its author's life is called an **autobiography.**

Nat Love wrote one of the most famous cowboy autobiographies. In his 1907 book, Love told many stories about his amazing life, and the book became very popular.

Love did not start life as a cowboy. He was born as an enslaved person in Tennessee in 1854 and he was freed after the Civil War ended. He wanted to go to school, but he could not find one. So when he was fifteen years old, he headed west.

Nat Love. *He wrote that he loved "the wild and free life of the plains."*

Bill Pickett. *This rodeo star invented bulldogging, which means jumping onto a steer and wrestling it to the ground.*

A Young Man Goes West

Love moved to Dodge City, Kansas, where he soon found a job as a cowboy that paid $30 a month. He soon became well-known for his skills at roping, riding, and taming horses.

Love had many adventures, and he also met other famous western heroes. For example, he knew Billy the Kid, Bat Masterson, and Frank and Jesse James.

He wrote about long cattle drives that he often took from Texas to Kansas. Love also fought wild animals and lived through harsh hailstorms, and he even claimed to have fourteen bullet wounds.

Love could not stay a cowboy for the rest of his life. After the railroad was built, fewer cowboys were needed because trains carried cattle across the country. Love took a job as a porter on the railroad, which means he carried passengers' luggage.

Rodeo Star

Love was not the only famous African American cowboy. Bill Pickett also left his mark on the West. He lived from 1870 to 1932, and he performed in shows called **rodeos** in which cowboys compete at dangerous tasks such as roping cattle and riding bulls.

Many rodeo events are very dangerous. Pickett broke nearly every bone in his body, but broken bones did not stop him. Pickett even went on to appear in two movies.

On the Range

Pickett and Love are just two of the thousands of famous African Americans from the Old West. Some others include Cherokee Bill, Jesse Stahl, Arthur L. Walker, Ben Hodges, Mary Fields, and Rufus Buck. Some were good guys and others were outlaws, but all of them helped settle the West. But history has forgotten them. Why?

Left Out of the Legend

Nat Love and Bill Pickett lived in times when real cowboys were real stars, but that changed. By the 1950s, most people learned about cowboys from popular books, movies, and TV shows.

These stories, called westerns, were not always true. Hardly any included African American cowboys, so people started to think that all cowboys were white. A key piece of American history had faded away.

Today we know better. People are retelling the stories of those long-forgotten cowboys, and that matters. After all, African Americans didn't just help build the Old West—they helped build America itself.

Wordwise

autobiography: book about its author's life

Civil War: conflict in the United States between 1861 and 1865

discrimination: unequal treatment

rodeo: cowboy show

You've heard of the cowboys of the Wild West, but have you ever heard of *gauchos*? Like their North American cousins, Argentine gauchos roamed the open plains. Find out how they survived in another wild land.

By Shirleyann Costigan

El Gauc

ho!

A stray cow breaks away from the herd and runs across the grasslands, and a man on horseback gallops after it. The horse turns sharply as it reaches the cow, and yet the rider sticks like glue on the horse's back. He twirls a woolen cloth in the air, which the rider uses to drive the stray cow back to the herd. Soon, they are lost in a cloud of dust kicked up by hundreds of pounding hooves.

Welcome to the world of the gaucho. Like the cowboy of America's Wild West, the gaucho of Argentina is tough and strong. He works long hours as a ranch-hand, he tames wild horses, and on long cattle drives, he might sleep on the ground, cook beef over an open fire, and drink bitter *maté* tea.

The Gaucho's Trail

The life of a gaucho is hard, and yet, to many in Argentina, the gaucho is a **folk hero**, and he is seen as noble and independent. Festivals and rodeos celebrate his history and traditions, and he is a symbol of national pride.

This was not always the case. Hundreds of years ago, the gaucho was a wanderer with no home. Even the word *gaucho* suggests a lonely life because it comes from words that mean "orphan" or "wanderer."

Over time, Argentina changed, and so did the gaucho and his image. The wanderer became a respected soldier, and the soldier became a restless ranch-hand. The ranch-hand became a hated outlaw, and finally, the outlaw became a celebrated folk hero. To see how the gaucho's image changed, let's follow his trail.

Wanderer of the Pampas

The gaucho's trail begins on the Pampas, the flat, grassy plains in central Argentina that the gaucho once ruled. Here, the open grasslands stretched as far as the eye could see, and strong winds howled across the bare landscape. It took a tough person to survive here. It took a gaucho.

Still, to the gaucho, the Pampas was more than a home. It was like a mother because it gave him what he needed to survive. He hunted wild cattle and birds for food and clothing, and he also captured wild horses.

The gaucho lived on his horse. In fact, he did everything on horseback, except sleep. He ate and even bathed on horseback! When he wasn't riding, the gaucho would say: "I am without feet."

The gaucho became known for his amazing ability to tame and ride horses. He used a saddle that had leather straps instead of stirrups for his feet. He rode across the plains bare-toed, gripping the straps between his first and second toes.

Survival Tools

After his horse, the gaucho's most prized possession was his *facón*, or knife, which he kept tucked in a belt at the small of his back. He used his razor-sharp knife to protect himself, as well as to kill and skin animals. He also cut giant slabs of meat with it to cook over an open fire. Then he used his knife like a fork to eat.

To catch animals, the gaucho used a lasso called *boleadoras*, or *bola* for short. He made it himself out of three strips of hide, or animal skin, and to the end of each, he tied a leather covered rock.

With the animal in sight, the gaucho whirled the bola above his head, faster and faster. It twirled and then, he let it fly. The three leather strips wound around the animal's legs, and the bola tripped it, so down it went.

On the open plains, weather often turned wet and cold, so to stay warm, the gaucho wore a wool blanket called a *poncho*. It covered his shoulders and kept him dry, and at night, he also slept on it.

Unlike the gauchos of the past, this gaucho uses stirrups and boots when riding his horse.

© JAVIER ETCHEVERRY/ALAMY

Gauchos are known for their riding skills. Here, a gaucho drives horses across a river.

From Wanderer to Soldier

Life for the early gauchos seemed simple and unchanging, and yet nothing ever stays the same. In the 1800s, three things happened that changed the gauchos' lives forever.

First, Argentina went to war with Spain in 1810. Spain had run Argentina for nearly 300 years, and now Argentina wanted to be independent. So gauchos became soldiers.

Their survival skills made them fierce fighters. They sent herds of cattle stampeding into enemy camps, they lassoed Spanish soldiers, and when under attack, they vanished into the grasslands.

From War Hero to Ranch-Hand

The gauchos helped win a war, and they also won respect. More ranchers began hiring gauchos to tend cattle. After all, the gauchos didn't need much. They were tough as nails, and they were fine cowboys.

In the early 1800s, the plains were wide open. **Descendants** of Spanish settlers built large *estancias*, or ranches. They used "living fences" such as trees or ditches to mark their fields. Their cattle roamed freely. So did the gauchos. Then another big change came in the 1840s. It changed ranch life—and the gauchos' lives.

This couple keeps gaucho tradition alive with a skirt-twirling dance.

From Ranch-Hand to Outlaw

The change came after one rancher visited England and saw how fences made it easier to raise **livestock** with fewer workers. He brought that idea back to Argentina. Soon, ranchers began stringing straight wire and barbed wire across the open grasslands.

Immigrants from Europe moved to the Pampas. They began farming, and they built fences, too. Over time, the open spaces all but disappeared.

Even as their world changed, the gauchos tried to stay the same. The ranchers didn't understand the gauchos' wandering ways. They said the gauchos broke the law by taking animals from their land, so the gaucho got a new name: outlaw.

From Outlaw to Hero

Few people wanted these outlaws around. Then the gauchos' image changed once more. In the 1870s, a poet wrote a long poem called "El gaucho Martín Fierro." It described one gaucho's life. It told how he loved freedom more than his belongings, and it told how he had been treated badly.

Thousands of Argentines read the poem, and the story touched their souls. They loved Fierro's independent spirit and admired his sense of honor and courage.

Thanks to this poem, once again the Argentine people respected the gaucho. His life was still hard, and yet now he was a hero not an outlaw. And so the legend of the gaucho was born.

Gauchos Today

If you take a trip to Argentina, you will see the gauchos of today. They may drive a pickup truck and live in a house. Some still work on ranches as cowboys; others have found city jobs.

Yet they keep the gaucho traditions alive with songs, poems, and dance. Shops sell silver knives, woven belts, and other crafts inspired by gauchos.

Gauchos show their horse-riding skills at rodeos and festivals. They lasso cattle, they ride bucking horses, and they also dance the *gato*, a gaucho dance for couples. They cook *asado*, slabs of beef, over a fire.

Meanwhile, deep in the Pampas, some gauchos still roam. Like their fathers and grandfathers before them, they live off the land and hold on to the old ways.

Can they survive in modern Argentina? No one knows, but one thing is certain: The gauchos, old and new, will fight to keep their traditions alive.

A son am I of the rolling plain
A gaucho born and bred,
And this is my pride: to live as free
As the bird that cuts through the sky.
        from "El gaucho Martín Fierro"

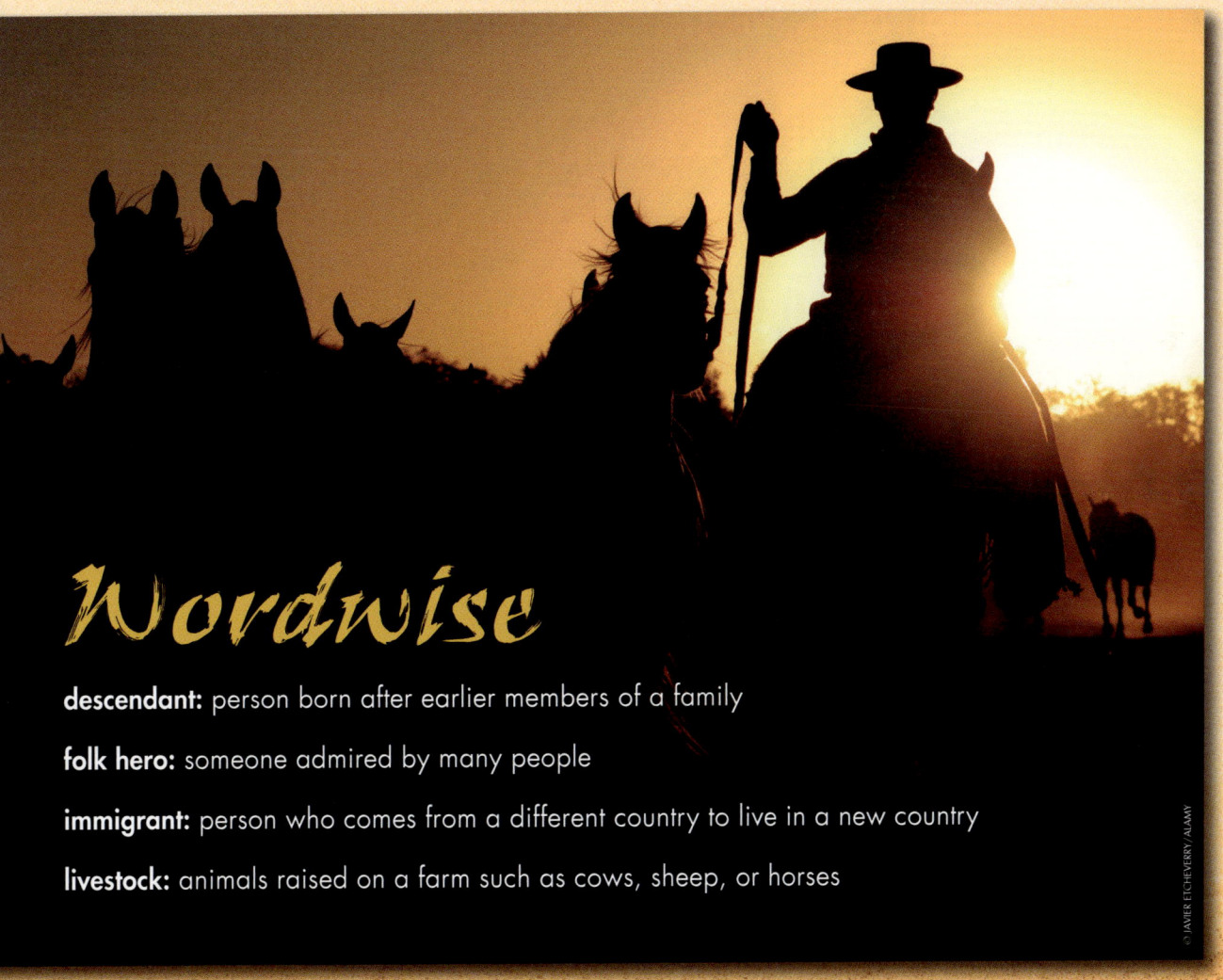

Wordwise

descendant: person born after earlier members of a family

folk hero: someone admired by many people

immigrant: person who comes from a different country to live in a new country

livestock: animals raised on a farm such as cows, sheep, or horses

COWBOYS

Ride away with the answers to these questions about cowboys.

1 Why did many African Americans move west after the Civil War?

2 How did books, movies, and television change people's image of cowboys in the United States?

3 Why did gauchos make good soldiers?

4 Picture a gaucho. What does he look like? What is he doing?

5 What is "wild" about a cowboy's life?